Great
Racing Cars

Great
Racing Cars

by George Sullivan

Illustrated with photographs

Dodd, Mead & Company   New York

Frontispiece: A race start at the Alabama International Motor Speedway, often hailed as the fastest track in stock car racing.

PICTURE CREDITS

Alabama International Motor Speedway, 2, 10, 25, Ron McQueeney, 15, 20; Daytona International Speedway, 24; Firestone, 54; International Hot Rod Association, D. Bishop, 42, David McGee, 43, 45; Aime LaMontagne, 8, 11, 12, 14, 16, 17, 18, 23, 37, 44, 50, 55, 56, 57, 59, 60, 61, 62; Long Beach Grand Prix Association, 32, 36, 39, 40; Michigan International Speedway, 22, 30; NASCAR, 26; Pocono International Raceway, 27; George Sullivan, 46, 47, 48, 49, 51, 52; Watkins Glen International, Randy McKee, 29; Watkins Glen Racing Museum, Tom Erwin, 31, 33.

Distributed in Canada by
McClelland and Stewart Limited, Toronto
Printed in Hong Kong by South China Printing Company

1 2 3 4 5 6 7 8 9 10

Library of Congress Cataloging-in-Publication Data
Sullivan, George, date
Great racing cars.
Includes index.
Summary: Describes a wide variety of racing cars and the races in which they are used.
1. Automobiles, Racing—Juvenile literature. [1. Automobiles, Racing.   2. Automobile racing]   I. Title.
TL236.S95   1987   629.2'28   87-8908
ISBN 0-396-08911-9

The author is grateful to the many people who contributed information and photographs used in this book. Special thanks are due: Bob Costanzo, Daytona International Speedway; Ron McQueeney, Indianapolis Motor Speedway; Neil Britt and Tammy Ferrell, National Hot Rod Association; John Evenson, CART; David McGee, International Hot Rod Association; Jim Freeman, Alabama International Motor Speedway; Ken Strobeck, Portland (Oregon) Rose Festival Association; Mike Clark, Road Atlanta; Bob Pleban, Pocono (Pennsylvania) Raceway; Herman Hickman, North Carolina Motor Speedway; Eric Dueweke and Anne M. Gilgallon, Detroit Grand Prix; Peter A. Biro, Long Beach Grand Prix Association; Karen Kurtz and Bill Green, Watkins Glen International; Donna Maxwell, Lime Rock (Connecticut) Park; Les Unger, New Jersey Sports and Exposition Authority; Dick Thompson, Martinsville (Virginia) Speedway; Darwin Doll, Michigan International Speedway; Louise Ann Noeth, Don Wigal, and Aime LaMontagne.

CONTENTS

INTRODUCTION

Automobile racing has come a long way since 1895 when the first real auto race took place on the dirt roads between Paris and Bordeaux in France, and back again. It covered a distance of 732 miles. The winner needed more than two *days* to finish. His average speed was 15.01 miles per hour.

Today, cars streak around tracks at speeds of more than 200 miles an hour. And whereas most early races attracted only a handful of curious onlookers, racing today draws more paying customers each year than baseball, basketball, or professional football.

One important reason for auto racing's popularity is the sport's variety. There's a type of racing to suit every taste. There are still road races, of course. They are not always run on ordinary roads, however. Cars compete on specially built road courses. These test drivers' skills on curves, sharp corners, and rolling hills.

Road racing is No. 1 in Europe. But Americans have always liked track racing best. With their long straightaways and sharply banked curves, modern tracks, called superspeedways, coax the fastest speeds possible out of cars.

The cars themselves take many forms, too. They range from battered jalopies that race on dirt tracks to high-speed stock cars. These look like ordinary passenger cars, but their engines have been torn down and rebuilt part by part to make them more powerful. Stock cars race fender-to-fender at speeds unthinkable for the family automobile.

Racing also includes small, low, and very fast Indy cars. They compete at the famed Indianapolis Speedway and more than a dozen other American tracks. They're piloted by some of the best-known drivers in the world.

Formula One cars look a great deal like Indy cars but they're designed to compete on road courses. Sometimes they're called Grand Prix cars.

Michael Andretti's Indy racer can speed along at 230 miles an hour on long straightaways.

Then there are sports cars. Some of these stress speed and cornering ability. With others, endurance is the key factor.

Dragsters are also a part of the American racing scene. Dragsters are cars that duel head-to-head over a distance of one-quarter of a mile. No car is faster than the Top-Fuel Dragster. One can cover a quarter of a mile in less time than it takes you to read this sentence.

This book examines the many different kinds of cars that make up American racing. It also puts the spotlight on the famous and historic races in which they compete.

Of course, the sport's variety is not the only reason that auto racing is so popular. The main reason is the sport itself. The sight and sound of powerful cars roaring down straightaways and whipping around sharp curves is always dramatic and exciting—and sometimes dangerous. Any sport with those ingredients is a hard sport to resist.

Track racing: Stock cars hurry through a high-banked turn at the Alabama International Motor Speedway, Talladega, Alabama.

1. INDY CARS

Small and low, with an open cockpit and no fenders, Indy cars are the fastest racing machines in the world. They can go from 0 to 60 miles an hour in two seconds, and from 0 to 100 mph in 4½ seconds.

Indy cars can blaze down track straightaways at speeds greater than 230 miles an hour. They're capable of lap averages of 216 miles an hour. No other cars in racing, including the famed Formula One racers can equal their speed.

It takes plenty of skill and experience to be

Indy cars—like this Lola/Cosworth piloted by Al Unser, Jr.—are the fastest racing machines in the world.

an Indy car driver. The Indy car is not a machine you hop into and take for a spin. "If you did that," says driver Kevin Cogan, "you'd have an accident every day."

The only way in which an Indy car resembles a car seen on city streets and highways is its use of tires and a steering wheel. Just about everything else is different.

Each Indy car is about 15 feet, 4 inches in length, and 6½ feet wide. Each weighs at least 1,550 pounds.

The frame that is attached to the axles and

Boxlike structure at the rear of the car, called a spoiler or wing, produces a downward force that holds the machine firmly to the track.

holds the body and motor, called the chassis (pronounced *chass-ee,* to rhyme with classy), is made of lightweight aluminum. A fiberglass "skin" covers the chassis and engine.

During the 1960s, Indy cars began using airfoils or spoilers. They're also called wings. But they're upside-down wings. Instead of providing lift, as an airplane wing does, the racing car wings produce a downward force, holding the car firmly to the road or track. This helps to boost the car's speed.

Indy cars race on very wide tires, each weighing about 28 pounds, which includes the weight of magnesium wheels. The tire surface is very thin; in fact, Indy tires are called "skin tires."

And they have no tread. Different types of tires are provided for each race, depending on the kind of track surface, concrete or asphalt.

Indy cars once had the engine in front. But rear-engine cars, introduced at the Indianapolis 500 in 1961, are what are seen today. In almost every case, the engines are built by Cosworth Engineering, a British company.

What makes the Indy car engine so powerful—they generate 750 horsepower, whereas a family automobile is usually rated at about 150 horsepower—is that it is equipped with a turbocharger. Referred to as a "blower" by drivers and mechanics, the turbocharger is a device that takes the engine's exhaust gases and uses them to drive a compressor that feeds air into the cylinders. The extra air helps the fuel burn more completely. More power is the result.

The driver has a control lever at his fingertips to regulate the turbocharger. When he wants a burst of speed, he moves the lever to force more air into the engine. But in so doing, he runs the risk of feeding so much air into the engine that it breaks down under the strain. You must have a delicate touch.

Indy cars run on powerful methyl alcohol, called methanol for short. They are anything but fuel-efficient. They average 1.8 miles per gallon. The average family car gets 25 to 35 miles per gallon.

Fuel tanks in Indy cars can be no bigger than 40 gallons. Tanks are made of rubberized nylon to prevent an explosion should the car crash.

Each year, Indy cars compete in a series of some fifteen races sponsored by CART (Championship Auto Racing Teams). Both track and road races, they range in distance from 100 to 500 miles.

In each race, the first driver to finish the required number of laps is the winner. (A lap is one complete circuit of the race track.) Drivers receive points based on how they finish in each race. The driver who wins the most points in a year is the United States driving champion.

During a race, cars must pull into the pits for fuel several times. (The pits are located on a roadway that runs parallel to the track's main straightaway.) On each pit stop, mechanics and crewmen have only seconds to refuel the car and perhaps change a tire or do minor mechanical work. Racing can easily be won or lost depending on how fast the pit crew works.

Events in the CART series include races at Phoenix, Milwaukee, Cleveland, and Miami; at the Meadowlands (in East Rutherford, New Jersey) and Brooklyn, Michigan; and at Montreal and Toronto in Canada.

Al Unser, Jr., waits patiently in his Lola/Cosworth as his pit crew performs their assigned chores.

The CART series also includes the Indianapolis 500, called the most important automobile race in the world. The Indianapolis 500 is held each Memorial Day, May 30, at the Indianapolis Speedway. There are 33 starting positions in the race. The first driver to complete the 200 laps around the paved, rectangular-shaped track—a distance of 500 miles—wins the race.

Drivers share the richest prize fund in auto racing. By the mid-1980s, the purse had reached $3 million. Recent winners have taken home more than half a million dollars.

To qualify for the race, each driver must compete in a series of trials held on the two weekends before the race. The 33 drivers with the fastest qualifying times line up in eleven rows, three cars to a row, at the race start.

The driver that sets the best four-lap average on the first day of qualifying wins the pole position. This is the position on the inside front at the beginning of the race. Because the inside position of the track offers the shortest distance around it, the pole position is a distinct advantage. Through 1986, twelve drivers had won the race from the pole position, from Johnny Murphy in 1922 to Bobby Unser in 1981.

The Indianapolis 500 was first run in 1911. It has been held every year since, except for two years during World War I and four years during World War II.

The track itself is even older than the race, having been built in 1909. Racing began in August that year. The main event was a 300-miler. The tar-and-gravel track was not able

The 1986 Indianapolis 500 gets underway. Tall tower at right center reports each car's position.

Geoff Brabham, behind the wheel of a Lola/Honda, hurries around a Meadowlands' turn.

to stand up to the pounding of the car's wheels, and began to break up. The race had to be halted after 235 miles.

In the months that followed, 3,200,000 bricks, each weighing ten pounds, were laid over the original surface. For years after, the Speedway was known as "the Brickyard," a nickname that's still heard. This is true even though the brick has been covered with asphalt. The paving job started in 1937 and reached final completion in 1976.

The track today is the same size it was in 1909: 50 feet wide on the straightaways and 60 feet wide on the turns.

Here are some other Indy facts:

• The Indy course is sometimes described as being "oval," but it's not. Many American tracks are true ovals, with banked U-turns at each end. But at Indy the turns are much tougher. Indy has 90-degree turns, two at each end. Each is a quarter mile long. That means on each circuit of the track there are four chances of making a mistake.

• About 400,000 people attend the race, although the count is never officially announced. About 235,000 fans sit along the course, and tens of thousands of others cram the infield or simply walk the grounds.

• Cars at Indianapolis usually make at least seven pit stops, although some drivers manage to squeak by on as few as six. Danny Sullivan, when he won in 1985, made eight.

• No more than five crewmen may work on a car during a pit stop. More than five earns the team a fine of $500.

• The largest number of rookie drivers occurred in 1919, when there were nineteen.

That's not counting 1911, when the first race was run and every driver was actually a rookie.

• A. J. Foyt and Al Unser, Sr., are the only drivers to have won four times at Indianapolis. Six drivers have won three times, including Johnny Rutherford, who was still racing into the late 1980s. A total of five drivers have won twice.

• Al Ulser, Sr., five days from his forty-eighth birthday, became the Speedway's oldest champion when he won the race in 1987. The youngest winner: Troy Ruttman. He was twenty-two when he won on his fourth try in 1952.

It takes special skills to be able to pilot a racing car that can tear along at 230 miles an hour. It takes experience, too. It used to be that drivers would prepare for Indy racing by driving midget racers or sprint cars on dirt and paved tracks. These cars, although smaller, handled somewhat like Indy cars. So it was not too difficult to move up to the "Big Cars," as Indy racers used to be called.

But modern Indy cars have little in common

Rick Mears (left) of Bakersfield, California, and Louisville's Danny Sullivan are among Indy racing's elite drivers.

17

with midgets and sprinters of the present day. There's a world of difference in how they handle.

Where do today's drivers get the training and experience they need to be able to drive Indy cars? Partly through the American Series. This consists of ten spring events, each 100 miles long. The Series features Wildcats, which are 400-horsepower, rear-engine, single-seat machines, developed by McLaren Engines of Livonia, Michigan.

The Super Vee Series is another training ground for future Indy car drivers. Super Vee cars are scaled-down versions of the Indy cars. The maximum weight of a Super Vee machine is 959 pounds (compared to 1,550 pounds for an Indy car). The Super Vee engine is rated at 190 horsepower. (The Indy car has a 750-horsepower engine.)

Super Vees compete in about a dozen races each year, sponsored by the Sports Car Club of America. In recent years, more than one-

Super Vee machines like this one are scaled-down versions of Indy cars.

third of the drivers competing in the Indy 500 have had Super Vee experience.

Racing at Indianapolis has led to many improvements in automobiles in general. For example, in their early years, passenger cars used up oil very fast. Some motorists had to buy a quart of oil for every five gallons of gas they purchased.

In the 1930s, a new rule at Indianapolis banned drivers from adding oil after the race had begun. Engineers went to work to develop engines that ran better on less oil—and they succeeded. These improvements were passed on to the auto industry. Today, an automobile runs for thousands of miles without the engine requiring additional oil.

Turbocharged engines, four-wheel brakes, and disc brakes were also pioneered at Indianapolis. A disc brake is one that stops a vehicle by means of friction generated between a set of rotating pads and a stationary disc. It is considered much superior to the drum brake, which was an auto industry standard for years.

High-traction tires were used on Indy cars for years before they were made available to owners of standard passenger cars. Indy car racing has also led to improved oils and other lubricants.

Speeds at Indianapolis climb steadily. Ray Harroun, who won in 1911 at the wheel of a Marmom, barely topped 80 miles an hour. Nowadays, the entire field averages over 200 miles an hour in qualifying.

The lap record at Indianapolis is 214.199 miles per hour. It was set in 1985 by twenty-six-year-old Scott Brayton of Coldwater, Michigan. Brayton was driving a turbocharged Buick V-6.

Bobby Rahal, behind the wheel of a March-Cosworth, sped to victory in 1986 in the fastest time in Indy history—170.722 miles per hour. It was one of the closest of all finishes. With two laps remaining and the cars traveling at a slow pace because of a yellow caution flag, Rahal was in second place behind Kevin Cogan. When the drivers got the green flag, Rahal was quick to react, charging ahead of Cogan to win by 1.44 seconds.

If there's any problem with Indy cars today, it may be that they're simply too fast. In the 1986 Michigan 500, held at the high-banked,

Bobby Rahal's pit crew flies into action during 1986 Indy 500. Rahal was eventual race winner.

two-mile-long International Speedway in Brooklyn, Michigan, only six of the 28 cars that started the race managed to finish it. Speed was the chief reason that 22 cars either broke down or crashed. Driver Bobby Rahal, who had won the Indy 500 earlier in the year, called the Michigan race a "demolition derby."

When a suspension piece failed on Mario Andretti's Lola at Michigan, his car pitched into a wall. "You just go along for the ride," Andretti said. "If the Almighty is away having lunch when it happens, you could be in a lot of trouble. I love to drive at Michigan but the speeds are horrifying now."

Said race winner Johnny Rutherford: "If we did something to slow the cars down, it would not make any of the drivers mad; it's worth a try."

Something was done. Engineers whose responsibility it was to write the Indy-car rules were just as concerned as many of the drivers. They rewrote the rules to reduce car speed. The major change was to decrease the size of the rear wing. This reduced the down-force produced by the wing. The result was less speed when rounding turns.

Not everyone agreed that change was necessary. "That's the name of the game in racing—go faster," said Ron Hamelgarn, who headed a race team at Michigan. "If they're scared, let them go home."

2. STOCK CARS

To most auto racing fans, Memorial Day weekend means the Indianapolis 500. The race and the date go together like October and the World Series or January and the Super Bowl.

But Memorial Day can mean something different in the southeastern United States. There, most racing fans focus their attention on the Charlotte Motor Speedway in Harrisburg, North Carolina, and the running of the World 600, one of the major events of the season in stock car racing. Since 1974, the World 600 has been run on the same day as the Indy 500.

More than 120,000 fans stand and cheer as the drivers take the green flag at the race start. "At Indianapolis, they draw 300,000," says H. A. Wheeler, president of the Charlotte Motor Speedway. "But if I had 300,000 seats, I could sell them."

The fans at Charlotte are among the many millions to whom auto racing means stock car racing. It's a sport that's as American as apple pie and Fourth of July fireworks.

Stock cars look like ordinary passenger cars. They have names that are very familiar to the American car owner—Chevrolet, Ford, Oldsmobile, Pontiac, and Buick. But the cars have been torn apart and rebuilt from the ground up to create power and speed.

This helps to explain the popularity of stock car racing. "Indy cars are designed by crew chiefs and engineers," says H. A. Wheeler. "Stock cars are designed for everyday people."

Stock car races are different, too. The cars are battlewagons, streaking along at speeds of 200 miles an hour and more, with drivers racing door to door. There's plenty of bumping and fender bending—but not necessarily wrecking.

"Watching Indy racing is something like watching pro football in a league where no-

Stock cars can streak along at speeds of 200 miles an hour and more.

body wears a helmet," says Wheeler. "You'd see a different kind of football. There wouldn't be much contact. Indy cars are small and very fast, but for safety reasons they can't race as close as stock cars."

The appeal of stock cars is not based only on all the "bammin' 'n jammin'" (banging fenders at very high speeds). Races are fiercely competitive. The lead changes hands on virtually every lap with cars traveling more than the length of a football field every second.

Stock car racing traces its beginnings to tracks laid out in cow pastures in the southern part of the United States. There were no real rules. Little was done to the cars to change

22

them into racing cars. They were truly "stock." As the cow pasture races increased in popularity, fans began to pay to watch.

The sport took a giant step forward in 1947. That was the year that a driver named Bill France organized a group of his fellow drivers into a club. They called the club the National Association for Stock Car Auto Racing, or NASCAR. Early in 1948, at Daytona Beach, Florida, NASCAR held its first race.

Today, NASCAR is one of the most powerful organizations in auto racing. It is also one of the most active. It sanctions more than 1,500 races a year. Prize money in NASCAR races totals some $15 million annually.

The cars that race in NASCAR events have to be "stock appearing"; that is, they must look like standard street automobiles. But special cams, rods, pistons, crankshafts, and other parts have been installed to boost the engine's power and speed. Exhaust systems have been modified; carburetors have been finely tuned.

The rules require that stock cars weigh 3,700 pounds; that's more than twice the weight of an Indy racer.

NASCAR modifieds duel wheel-to-wheel at the Stafford Motor Speedway, Stafford Springs, Connecticut.

All stock cars must have a 100-inch wheelbase. (The wheelbase is the distance between the front and rear axles.)

Stock cars are not allowed to use automatic transmissions. Instead, the driver shifts gears by means of a standard manual transmission.

Getting a car ready to race on the NASCAR circuit can be very costly, with the price tag running as high as $60,000. About one-quarter of the cost, or $15,000, goes for the car's engine.

A great many of the best cars have been

built by Junior Johnson and his fifty-five employees at Junior Johnson Associates of Ingle's Hollow, North Carolina. Johnson's racing teams, through 1985, had won 119 races and six of the previous ten NASCAR driving championships. Other outstanding cars have been built by Banjo Matthews, Cotton Owens, and Hutcherson-Pagan of Charlotte.

The leading stock car drivers are household names. When fans refer to "Richard," "David," "Cale," or "Bobby," they mean Richard Petty, David Pearson, Cale Yarborough, and Bobby Allison.

Richard Petty, from Randleman, North Carolina, is a stock car racing legend. He won more than 200 races in a career that covered more than three decades. Petty's 200th win came on July 4, 1984, in the Firecracker 500 at Daytona. President Ronald Reagan was in the stands that day. Petty's son, Kyle, who became a driver on the NASCAR circuit in 1979, won more than a million dollars in prize money.

Cars get the starting flag at the Daytona International Speedway.

David Pearson, from Spartanburg, South Carolina, a three-time national driving champion, was second to Richard Petty in number of wins. He had more than 100 of them.

Cale Yarborough's career, like Richard Petty's, covered over thirty years. "I think of myself as good wine," Yarborough once said. "The older, the better." Yarborough, who hailed from Sardis, South Carolina, chalked up almost 100 career victories.

Bobby Allison, from Hueytown, Alabama, also had close to 100 career wins. One of the most competitive drivers of all time, Allison bounced from team to team in an effort to find the winning combination of car and crew chief. In terms of popularity, Allison had few rivals. Seven times fans voted him "Most Popular Driver."

These four drivers were typical in that they all came from the South. They also all were racing into their forties, which is not unusual in stock car competition. And Pearson was still at it in his fifties.

Cale Yarborough and his Hardee's Ford lead the pack at the Alabama International Motor Speedway.

A complicated system of scoring is used in determining the year's top driver. The system has often been criticized. It is said to favor those drivers who do well in the most races, not necessarily those who win the most races. For example, Bill Elliott was thought by most observers to be the No. 1 driver in 1985. He won eleven races, a record. He earned more than $2 million in prize money.

Yet Elliott finished second to Darrell Waltrip in the point standings. Waltrip won only three races and about half as much prize money as Elliott. But Waltrip was among the top ten finishers 20 times; Elliott, 18 times. Even Waltrip called the method of choosing the year's outstanding driver a "bad" system.

Stock cars race on several different types of tracks: short tracks, which are less than a mile around, oval tracks, and tri-ovals. A tri-oval is a D-shaped course which can be as long as 2.66 miles. Stock cars also compete on two road courses—at Riverside, California, and Watkins Glen, New York.

Besides the World 600 at Charlotte, NAS-CAR offers three other "Crown Jewel" races

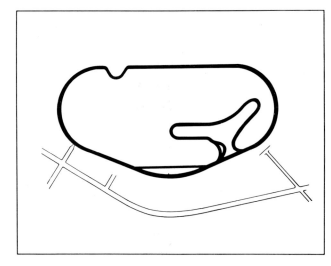

Daytona (Florida) International Speedway, a 2.5-mile tri-oval.

each year. These are: the Daytona 500 (held at the Daytona International Speedway in Daytona Beach, Florida), the Southern 500 (held at the Darlington International Speedway in Darlington, South Carolina), and the Talladega 500 (held at the Alabama International Speedway in Talladega, Alabama).

Each of these race courses has its own special character. The Daytona track, for example, is recognized as the world's most famous high-banked superspeedway. Cars whiz their way around the 2.5-mile tri-oval at speeds that average close to 175 miles an hour. In the infield, there's Lake Lloyd, a man-made lake. From the huge pit that forms the lake, the dirt was taken to build Daytona's high-banked turns.

For the Daytona 500, the first big event of the year on the NASCAR calendar, more than 100,000 fans show up. The prize fund for the race, first run in 1959, is more than $1 million.

Darlington Raceway has been described as "the track that's too tough to tame." The 1.366-mile oval is tight and tricky. Races are usually won through driver ability—or lost through driver error. "There's nothing easy about it," says Darrell Waltrip.

The Alabama International Speedway at Talladega is a 2.66-mile tri-oval. Built in 1968, it is the biggest and fastest of the superspeedways. When Bill Elliott turned in a qualifying time of 209.398 mph at Talladega in 1985, he set a world speed record for stock cars.

In the pits at these and other tracks, drivers, their crew members, and other insiders use

A pit stop for Harry Gant's Skoal Bandit Chevrolet at the Pocono (Pennsylvania) International Raceway.

special words and terms to describe their cars and what they've done to them. Here is a sampling of what you are likely to hear:

Air dam—The horizontal piece molded around the front of the car beneath the bumper. It prevents air from passing beneath the car and creating lift. Lift works to slow down the car. It can even cause the driver to lose control.

Spoiler—The winglike section that is bolted horizontally across the car's trunk. It works to push down on the back of the car, creating better traction for the rear wheels.

Sidepods—The pieces on the sides of the car that house the radiator and also control the air flow.

Stagger—The difference in the size of the tires on the right and left sides. On an oval track made up of four left-hand turns, for example, the tires on the right side are larger in circumference than those on the left side. This helps to balance the car as each turn is made.

Dialed-in—Getting the car tuned up perfectly for a particular track.

Engine let-go—An internal breakdown. Oil, water, and broken parts may spill from the car, creating a dangerous situation on the track.

Drafting—The practice of driving close behind another car to take advantage of the reduced air resistance just in back of it. The front car punches a "hole" in the air. The trailing car is able to travel at the same speed as the lead car while using less fuel. To some extent, it is "towed" by the first car.

In recent years, NASCAR officials have been trying to make the sport more national in its appeal. This means scheduling races outside the Southeast. But the problem is that there happens to be only a handful of large oval tracks outside of the Southeast. The solution has been to race stock cars on road courses.

A road course can present special problems for stock car drivers. Take, for instance, the road circuit at Watkins Glen, New York. Its 3.377 miles of asphalt wind through the tree-covered hills at the southern tip of New York's Seneca Lake. The circuit includes seven corners, some right, some left. (On a track, there

Racing action at the famed road course at Watkins Glen, New York.

are only left turns.) Speeds on the back straight hit 180 miles an hour.

Racing on a steep-banked oval is something like driving fast on an interstate highway. But competing at Watkins Glen is like racing on a country road. Sports cars take to road circuits naturally. They're about half the weight of the average stock car and are much easier to maneuver. Stock cars have to be wrestled around the tricky turns. And drivers have to shift gears almost constantly as they speed up, brake for a turn, then speed up again.

The idea of stock cars racing at Watkins Glen and other road circuits has proven appealing. But no one doubts that "real" stock car racing is what takes place at Daytona, Darlington, Charlotte, and Talladega. That's where the bulky sedans cruise in heavy traffic at speeds about 200 miles an hour. That's where crowds often bigger than 100,000 turn out. That's where stock car racing takes off in America.

Cars pour out of the long straight into a turn at the Michigan International Speedway.

3. FORMULA ONE RACERS

Imagine a car that looks something like an Indy racer, a small, slim single-seater, low to the ground with no fenders. It's been stripped of everything except a gearbox, a fuel tank, an engine, wheels, and brakes. Built to run on road courses, it is lightning fast on straightaways but can slow down to a crawl on hairpin turns.

Such a car is no fantasy. It's the Formula One racer, a racing sports car. (It is called a Formula One car because it is built according to a "formula," a set of specifications drawn

Smaller than Indy cars, Formula One racers are slim single-seaters built to race on rugged road courses.

up by the FISA, the Federation Internationale du Sport Auto, located in Paris.)

The cars that race at Indianapolis and other CART events have only one useful gear. One is all they require. And they can be steered only around left-hand turns. While the Indy car is sleek and very fast, it would be useless even for a trip to the supermarket. But the Formula One machine has four or five speeds forward, can turn right as well as left, and do anything else a sports car can do.

All Formula One engines are 1.5-liter turbo-charged units. The rules limit engine power to 600 horsepower. (The standard family automobile delivers about 150 horsepower.) The limit for Formula One machines used to be 800 horsepower, but the amount was reduced in 1986 to improve safety.

Formula One cars are not permitted to carry any more than forty gallons of fuel. Races are usually 150 to 250 miles long, and the fuel has to last the entire race. Under present rules, there are no pit stops for refueling in Formula One racing.

As a result, a driver cannot have a "heavy foot" on the gas pedal. If he did, he would use up his fuel before the race ended. He has to handle the car carefully in an effort to get the most miles-per-gallon possible.

Some car manufacturers have solved this problem through the use of electronic fuel injection systems. These feed the fuel to the engine as economically as possible, and do so automatically. All the driver has to do is drive.

Racing a Formula One car for a full season is very expensive. *Car and Driver* magazine says the cost begins at about $10 million and can range up to twice that amount.

Formula One cars are sleek and fast, and can do anything a sports car can do.

It's mostly European car manufacturers that have been willing to bear this expense. Formula One racers are German BMWs and Porsches, Italian Ferraris and Alfa Romeos, French Renaults, and British Lolas. (There are also Hondas from Japan.)

In the mid-1980s, however, an American name—Ford—began to be heard. Lolas built in England were powered by a new engine, a turbocharged Ford V-6. The engine was designed in England by Keith Duckworth and built by Duckworth's company, Cosworth Engineering.

Cosworth is a name well known in racing circles. A Cosworth Ford V-8 once dominated Grand Prix racing. A turbocharged Cosworth Ford was what powered Bobby Rahal's car when he won the Indianapolis 500 in 1986.

Formula One racers compete on what is known as the Grand Prix circuit, and sometimes they're called Grand Prix cars. (Prix, pronounced *pree,* is the French word for prize.) The Grand Prix consists of approximately fifteen races run on rugged road tracks, each several miles in length. The races are from 150 to 250 miles long. The first driver to finish the required number of laps wins.

The fifteen races are held in western Europe, South America, South Africa, Australia, the

John Watson driving a Brabham/Cosworth BT 44 in the 1974 U.S. Grand Prix at Watkins Glen, New York.

United States, and Canada. In North America, race sites have included Watkins Glen, New York, and Long Beach, California, where cars race on a course laid out through city streets. In recent years, Grand Prix fans have had a chance to see Formula One cars and drivers compete at the Canadian Grand Prix in Montreal and the Detroit Grand Prix, which is also run on city streets.

About a dozen Grand Prix events are held on European road courses each year. While track races are the most popular type of automobile races in the United States, Europe has always favored road races. Sometimes they are roads or streets that are normally public. Other times they are specially built.

The European races have included the Dutch Grand Prix at Zandvoort, the German Grand Prix at Nürburgring, the Italian Grand Prix at Monza, and the Monaco Grand Prix through the streets of Monte Carlo.

The Belgian Grand Prix is raced on a track that is a good example of the European road course. Located deep in the Ardennes Forest of western Belgium, the track is named Spa-Francorchamps. Spa is the closest town to the track. Francorchamps is the closest village. The track is called Spa for short.

The Belgian Grand Prix was first run at Spa in 1925. In those days, the roadways winding through the forests, hills, and meadowlands were narrow and bumpy, the hills steep and the curves very sharp. Over the years, conditions were improved little by little, chiefly by smoothing and widening the roads. Spa eventually became an 8.7-mile road course that was shaped more or less like a triangle, its sides bent in a few places.

The course had long straights where cars could hit speeds of 170 miles an hour for minutes at a time. There were hairpin turns at the end of the straights where speeds had to cut back to 120 miles an hour or less. And there were about thirty often scary turns.

The race was usually decided on the turns. The skilled and experienced drivers would take each turn at very close to the maximum speed possible. But the less skilled and experienced drivers slowed down on the turns, so as not to spin out of control. Almost always, the Belgian Grand Prix was won by great drivers.

Formula One cars hurry through a crowded turn at the Long Beach Grand Prix.

As Formula One cars became more powerful, Spa was judged to be too dangerous for them. Racing ended at Spa in the early 1970s.

But during the mid-1980s, with Formula One racing enjoying a spurt in popularity, Spa was opened again. The circuit was shortened to about four miles and the roadway paved with a rubberized asphalt that made for a very grippy surface. *Car and Driver* magazine said the course had been "safety-ized." But what had been done did not really change the character of the course. The magazine called it "breathtaking . . . the world's greatest natural road course."

In each Grand Prix race, the drivers receive points based upon where each finishes. The driver who earns the most points in a year wins the World Driving Championship, the most coveted title in auto racing.

Since 1950, the year the title was first awarded, only two Americans have been able to lay claim to the championship. One was Phil Hill, who won the championship in 1961; the other was Mario Andretti, one of American racing's all-time greats.

Born in Florida, Phil Hill grew up in California and owned his first car, a second-hand Ford Model-T, at the age of twelve. He was racing at thirteen and began driving Ferrari sports cars in 1956 at twenty-nine. Before long, he moved up to Formula One Ferraris.

Hill won his first Grand Prix event at Monza in northern Italy in 1960. He averaged 132 miles an hour, a record for the track.

It was at Monza, too, that Hill captured the world title in 1961. The race was marred by tragedy. Hill entered Monza in second place in the standings for the championship. He had 29 points. Germany's Count Wolfgang Graf Berghe von Trips was the leader with 33 points. A gaunt, hatchet-faced man, von Trips had a long record of accidents. His nickname was "Count Crash."

As the race got underway, Hill grabbed the lead. Von Trips got caught in the pack. As the cars moved through a tree-shrouded turn and into the long, back straight, von Trips began to weave his way through the cluster of speeding cars. He passed Jack Brabham and then moved on Jimmy Clark. But as he tried to ease past Clark, von Trips' rear wheel brushed a front wheel of Clark's car. Both machines spun out of control.

Clark's car came to a stop near the track edge. Von Trips' was not so fortunate. His car slammed hard into a guard rail, glanced off Clark's car a second time, and then hurtled into the spectator area. Von Trips was thrown from his car and killed. Fourteen spectators also died.

The race continued. Hill knew there had been a crash but he had no idea how serious it was. One by one, Hill's challengers dropped away. When he crossed the finish line, Hill was all smiles. He was still grinning when he received his championship trophy. When he was finally told what had happened, his face turned white and he sat stunned, unable to speak.

Mario Andretti won the World Driving Championship in 1978. He scored victories that year in Grand Prix races in Argentina, Belgium, Spain, France, and Holland.

Andretti was claimed not only by America's racing fans but by those of Italy, too. He was born in 1940 in Trieste, Italy, on the Adriatic Sea. The family lost everything during World

Mario Andretti, a frequent winner in Indy car competition, was also a championship performer on the Formula One circuit.

War II, and lived in a camp for displaced persons for seven years. The Andrettis emigrated to America in 1955, settling in Nazareth, Pennsylvania.

Mario developed his driving skills in beat-up jalopies, tricky midgets, and powerful sprint cars. His relentless, charging way of driving caused him to crash fairly regularly in his early years. He eventually toned down his ferocious style and went on to win just about every race worth winning.

He won the Indy car championship four times—in 1965, 1966, 1969, and 1984. Through the season of 1985, he had scored 45 Indy car victories. He captured U.S. Driver of the Year honors three times—in 1967, 1978, and 1984.

Today, Andretti lives on Victory Lane in Nazareth with wife, Dee Ann, their daughter Brenda Dee, and their two sons, Michael and Jeff. By the late 1980s, both sons were beginning to distinguish themselves in American auto racing.

Mario Andretti and Phil Hill are rare exceptions. The best drivers on the Formula One circuit are almost always Europeans or South Americans. Jackie Stewart, from Scotland, and nicknamed the Wee Scot, was one. Stewart was a shrewd driver who seldom abused his cars. And he was also very safety conscious.

Stewart won the World Driving Championship in 1969, 1971, and 1973, the year he retired. He was thirty-four at the time.

How good was Jackie Stewart? Consider this: He competed in 99 Formula One races and he won 27 times. No other driver won as many races as Stewart.

Austrian Nikki Lauda was another outstanding Grand Prix driver in recent years. He won the World Championship in 1975, 1977, and 1984.

Lauda is known as a highly intelligent driver. "His brain is always ticking away like a Rolex," said a friend. "He's always weighing the odds, considering the options."

Lauda once disclosed his "secret" for his success in these words: "I do what I always do. Take it easy in the early laps, then find my way through, then do the job."

During the mid-1980s, Alain Prost, a French driver, began to challenge the accomplishments of Nikki Lauda and Jackie Stewart. Prost, in 1985, became the first Frenchman to win

the World Driving Championship. He clinched the title in the Grand Prix of Europe, held at Brands Hatch, England. He won the title a second time in 1986.

Prost was fourteen when he entered his first race. It was in Cannes, France, where he was vacationing with his parents and older brother, Daniel. In that race, Prost drove a go-kart, a very small vehicle with a power mower-type gasoline engine. Although he had a broken arm because of an accident in soccer, Alain won easily, beating eighteen other starters.

In 1972, at the age of seventeen, Prost won the European go-kart championship. He was the French Renault champion in 1977. He became the Formula Three title-holder in 1979. A year later, he entered his first Formula One race, the Grand Prix of Argentina. Eighteen months later, he won his first Formula One event, capturing the French Grand Prix.

Prost is a natural behind the wheel; he makes the job look easy. He never bullies the car. He goes into turns early, brakes late, and never

Formula One cars are lightning fast on straightaways but can slow down to a crawl on tight turns.

39

lets the rear end get very much out of line.

By 1986, Prost had won 23 Formula One events. He was thirty-one; his best driving years were ahead of him. The chances seemed excellent that he would top Jackie Stewart's record of 27 lifetime wins.

During the mid-1980s, Eddie Cheever was the only American driving on the Grand Prix circuit. It did not seem likely that Cheever would replace Prost or Lauda at the top of the heap. His performance in the Detroit Grand Prix in 1986 was not untypical. While Cheever did manage to qualify in a new Ford Formula One, he was not able to finish the race. Ayrton Senna, a twenty-six-year-old Brazilian, driving a Lotus, emerged as champion.

Extra-wide trackless tires are a leading feature of Grand Prix Formula One machines.

4. DRAGSTERS

Drag racing has always been a simple sport. Cars race two at a time. They both line up at the starting line and take off on a given signal. The first dragster to cross the finish line, exactly one-quarter of a mile (1,320 feet) away, wins.

Cars reach speeds of more than 270 miles an hour in less than six seconds. Or look at it this way: A dragster can cover the length of a football field in the time it takes you to blink your eyes.

The dragster goes so fast that its rear-wheel brakes aren't enough. It needs a parachute to help slow it down.

For spectators, drag racing offers special thrills. When the starting light flashes green and the dragsters rocket away, the engine noise batters your eardrums. If you're not wearing earplugs—most fans do—your head buzzes like someone is running an electric mixer inside it. Your body shivers. If you happen to be sitting in a wooden grandstand, the sound waves vibrate the seat and tickle your backside.

One spectator described it in these terms: "Lean over the fence, and the afterblast skins your forehead, singes your nostril hairs, and polishes your teeth."

The noise isn't the only thing that makes drag racing unusual. It's one of the few sports in which fans are allowed to mix with the contestants. In fact, mixing is encouraged. Crowds are permitted to stroll through the sprawling pit area where the cars are being prepared for the next run. You can watch last-second adjustments being made; you can talk with the drivers and mechanics. It's like visiting a baseball locker room and interviewing the players just before they take the field.

In the early days of drag racing during the 1930s, "hot rodders," as the drivers were then called, raced almost anywhere there was a flat

To slow down and stop, dragsters need, besides brakes, the aid of a parachute.

and open space. Their cars were usually stripped-down Model-Ts or Model-A Fords.

The sport owes much to a former driver named Wally Parks. The friendly, outgoing Parks helped to start *Hot Rod Magazine,* the "bible" of the sport, in 1948. Three years later, Parks founded the National Hot Rod Association (NHRA), which brought order to the sport.

The NHRA sanctioned races and helped to boost safety standards. The organization ruled that all cars must be fitted with roll bars. These are heavy steel bars that curve over the driver to form a cage that helps to protect him should the car flip over. NHRA said that drivers must wear crash helmets. The organization also ordered that cars be fitted with clutch shields and flywheel shields. In case either explodes, the shield helps to keep the parts contained.

Today, the NHRA conducts more than 2,000

drag-racing events in the United States and Canada each year. Millions of fans attend these races. Many of these people are competitors themselves, so-called "weekend warriors," racing on local tracks.

Among these events is a season-long series of races matching the best cars and drivers. The series begins in February with the Winter Nationals in Pomona, California, and ends at the same place with the World Finals in October. In between, there are a dozen other stops—at Atlanta and Phoenix; at Baton Rouge, Louisiana; Bowling Green, Kentucky; and Mohnton, Pennsylvania, to name a few of them.

The biggest drag-racing event of them all takes place over Labor Day weekend at the U.S. Nationals at Indianapolis Raceway Park in Clermont, Indiana. The NHRA has been running its championships at Indy for more than twenty-five years.

"The Nationals are a special attraction," *Car and Driver* magazine noted recently. "The joint

Top Fuel Dragsters, Funny Cars, and Pro Stockers await the call to action in track staging area.

The Top Fuel Dragster is made up of huge tires and a monster engine at the rear that are connected by a long, thin chassis to smallish front wheels.

is packed with every kind of nutball car you can imagine, from sixties muscle cars to 3,000 hp, nitro-burning rolling hand grenades . . ." More than 600 cars in a variety of classes compete at the Nationals.

What most spectators at the Nationals and other events along the NHRA circuit go to see are the Top Fuel Dragsters, Pro Stockers, and Funny Cars. The Top Fuel Dragster is the fastest of the three types. It consists of a pair of huge tires, a monster engine, and a seat for the driver. These are linked by a spidery framework of metal tubing to smallish front wheels. The machine looks like something you'd build with a Tinker Toy set.

These cars are called "Top Fuel" because they run on nitromethane, a fuel more powerful than gasoline. In fact, there's no fuel hotter than nitro.

The Top Fuel Dragster's enormous engine

is capable of producing as much as 3,000 horsepower. That's about four times as much as an Indy car and about twenty times as much as the average family automobile.

The huge rear tires are made of a special soft and almost gummy rubber that helps them grip the track. Just before the race, drivers "burn out" their tires. They spin them furiously on the track. The burnout heats the tires and creates even more traction.

During the burnout, white smoke billows from the spinning tires and the stench of burning rubber fills the air. Specks of rubber are thrown from the tires like raindrops. You get showered if you stand too close.

After the burnout, each car makes a short practice run. This is called a "dry-hop." Its purpose is to heat up the clutch.

Drivers then return to the starting line. Each gets the signal to go from watching the Christmas tree—an electronically controlled system of lights mounted to a tall pole. The Christmas tree stands between the two racing strips just beyond the starting line.

First, on each side of the pole at the very top, two amber lights flash. These are the

All dragsters "burn out" their tires before a race. This is Funny Car driver Jim Head in his Oldsmobile Firenza.

"prestaged" lights. They're a signal to each driver that his or her car is close to the starting line.

Next, as each car gets set for its run, another pair of amber lights blinks on. These are the "staged" lights. Their message is that each car is ready for its run.

With the staged lights on, and tension at its peak, five amber countdown floodlights begin to flash in sequence from top to bottom. Four-

45

Electronically controlled stack of lights—called a Christmas tree—signals race start.

tenths of a second after the bottommost amber floodlight has gone on, the green light flashes— and the cars roar off.

One second the dragsters are sitting there, each creating as much noise and excitement as World War II, and the next second, they're gone. It takes less than four seconds for a car to go from zero to 200 miles per hour.

At the end of the strip, electronic eyes decide which car has crossed the finish line first and measures the speed of each vehicle. This information is instantly flashed to the spectators.

Among the drivers of Top Fuel Dragsters, there are two whose names rank above all others—Don (Big Daddy) Garlits and Shirley Muldowney. Garlits, who turned fifty-five in 1987, is a drag racing legend. He has been regarded as King of the Hot Rodders for almost thirty years.

In 1985, Garlits won six NHRA National events, more victories in a single season than any other Top Fuel driver in history. When Garlits won the U.S. Nationals at Indianapolis in 1986, it marked his thirty-third career win.

Along the way, Garlits set a helmetful of speed records. In 1964, he was the first driver to exceed 200 miles an hour. Later, Garlits was the first to top 250 and 260. In the spring of 1986, at Gainesville, Florida, he became the first driver to edge past 270 miles per hour.

Much of the progress in professional drag

Among drivers of Top Fuel Dragsters, Don (Big Daddy) Garlits reigned as king for years.

racing has resulted from changes pioneered by Big Daddy himself. For many years, top fuel dragsters had their engines in front of the driver. Big Daddy was the first to build a successful rear-engine car. That was in 1972. Today, all top-fuel dragsters are rear-engined.

Garlits was the first to mount a wing at the rear of the car. Once the car is underway, the wing acts to increase the traction of the rear wheels. The greater the traction, the more speed.

Garlits also helped to develop the fire-resistant suit all drivers now wear. In 1986, he replaced the usual dragster front wheels, 18 inches in diameter, with tiny 13-inch wheels. Instead of having tires, each wheel was fitted with a rubber belt.

The success of Shirley Muldowney—often called the First Lady of the drag strips—the NHRA's only three-time world champion in Top Fuel, stemmed more from talent than from any technical advances. Muldowney believed that her hands did much to make her successful. "It takes a light touch in a rail," she once said. "It really does. You've got all of this incredible power, but you get up and

This 3,000-horsepower engine enabled Big Daddy Garlits to surpass 270 miles per hour.

you start manhandling and being a savage and a brute; that doesn't get the job done."

When she drove, Muldowney wore driving mittens rather than gloves. She said the mittens enabled her to feel her fingers and gave her even more in the way of touch. "I'm not sure if you'd call it a woman's touch or not," she said. "But I do think that women have better reflexes." In her own case, that statement was certainly true. In race after race, Shirley was the driver who got away quickest at the start.

While Top Fuel Dragsters are the most unusual looking machines you'll see in auto racing, Pro Stock cars most closely resemble the cars to be found on city streets. They are alike in many ways. Each Pro Stocker has the same basic engine and the same body as the car it appears to be. But it has been worked on to produce the fastest possible speed for the one-quarter of a mile run.

The Pro Stocker is usually a Ford or Chevrolet, although occasionally racers choose a Chrysler, Pontiac, Oldsmobile, or Buick. Every car must have a roll-bar cage to protect the driver and a parachute to aid in stopping.

The rules permit fiberglass or other lightweight material to be used for the hood, front fenders, rear deck, and some other parts. But each must be the exact size and shape of the part replaced. The original length and width of the car must remain the same. One change that is permitted is the use of hood air scoops.

The air scoop helps to get more air into the engine, cooling it.

As with Top Fuel Dragsters, success or failure in Pro Stocker races is usually decided in terms of hundredths of a second. "We know we're not allowed to make an error," says Bob Glidden, who set a record in 1986 by winning his seventh U.S. Pro Stock title. "If we make an error, we lose."

Top Fuel Dragsters may be the fastest of the dragsters and Pro Stockers may look the most like street-driven automobiles, but the stars at every track are the Funny Cars. Their fiberglass bodies somewhat resemble those of standard cars, such as the Chevrolet Camaro or Corvette, the Ford Thunderbird or Tempo, or the Pontiac Trans-Am. But Funny Cars are shorter, have long noses, fat tails, and assorted bulges in the wrong places.

The name "funny" for the class goes back to the 1960s. That's when drag racers would take stock cars and move the rear wheels forward, raise the nose, and make other changes

Shirley Muldowney, three-time champion in Top Fuel competition

Pro Stocker's front wheels are wrenched from the ground during a "dry hop."

Funny Cars are short, have long noses and fat tails.

that were meant to urge more speed out of the vehicle. These cars looked unusual. "Funny cars" are what they were called, and the name stuck. Eventually a separate class was created for them.

While they may be called funny, there's nothing laughable about the way in which they perform. They're brute force, a fist in the face. Under the fiberglass body shell, there's a 2,000-horsepower engine that gulps nitromethane, the same propellant used by Top Fuel Dragsters. Each Funny Car has a supercharger intake mounted on the hood. It forces more air into the engine for greater power. The result is that Funny Cars are almost as fast as Top Fuelers, achieving speeds beyond 250 miles an hour.

The driver sits behind the engine where the rear seat would ordinarily be. He or she wears a heavy, fire-resistant suit and uses a special breathing apparatus that filters out poisonous fumes that can build up inside the car. A firewall separates the driver and the engine.

Funny Cars are doorless. Fiberglass body shell must be raised to permit the driver to enter and exit.

Two small windows are built into the wall. These enable the driver to see the engine and spot flames should they begin burning.

On-board computers are the latest wrinkle in Funny Car design. Kenny Bernstein, who has many runs over 260 miles an hour, used a computer. "It'll tell us the engine revolutions, acceleration, amount of clutch slippage, and when the transmission shifts," Bernstein explained. Such information tells clearly how the car is running.

To many people, drag racing once meant kids in black leather jackets with slicked-back hair racing one another on suburban roads long after dark. That image is fast going the way of the Volkswagon bug and the five-cent telephone call. Today, drag racing means highly skilled men and women professionals who duel in expensive, high-powered cars at speeds unknown even at such sites as Indianapolis and Daytona.

Top Fuel Dragsters are not only powerful and fast, they're colorful, too.

5. OTHER CARS, OTHER RACERS

When it comes to auto racing in America, the newspaper headlines usually go to the sleek Indy speedsters or the fast Formula One racers. Or they feature the powerful stock cars that ply the high-banked turns at Charlotte and Daytona Beach and the like.

But the truth is that racing in the United States runs much broader and deeper than the headlines suggest. It also includes hundreds of events for amateur and professional drivers that are sponsored by the Sports Car Club of America (SCCA) and the International Motor Sports Association (IMSA). Almost all of these are run on road circuits, but a handful are held on courses that combine the features of a road course and oval track.

The chief goal of the SCCA is "to further the . . . operation of sports cars, and provide events for these cars and their owners."

What is a "sports car," anyway? The first sports cars were simply spiffy, two-seat, high-performance automobiles that were meant for everyday driving on public roads. They were smaller and lighter than ordinary passenger cars.

They also had racing car features. These included wonderfully responsive controls and the ability to accelerate fast. All in all, sports cars made driving fun.

The *racing* sports car is a little bit different. It's a sleek two-seat, open-cockpit car with a body that covers the wheels. Although the cockpit is designed to permit seating for two, it has only a driver's seat. Normal highway equipment, such as headlights and windshield wipers, are not used. It has an extremely powerful engine.

Racing organizations still provide competition for the traditional type of sports car. But they have added many other categories. GT—

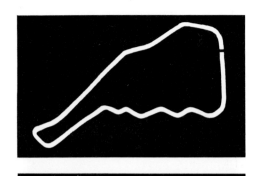

Nation's best-known road circuits include:

Road Atlanta
(Gainesville, Georgia)
2.52 miles

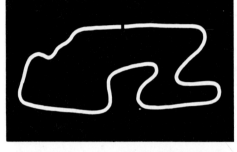

Watkins Glen
International
(Watkins Glen, New York)
3.77 miles

Road America
(Elkhart Lake, Wisconsin)
4.0 miles

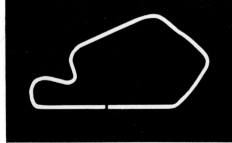

Lime Rock Park
(Lime Rock, Connecticut)
1.52 miles

for Grand Touring—cars are one. GT cars are manufactured for sale to the public and can be entered in certain types of races.

There are also GTP cars. GTP stands for Grand Touring Prototype. Unlike GT cars, wherein a certain number must be built in order to qualify for racing, a GTP car is simply a specially built racing sports car.

GT cars are also sometimes designated GTO or GTU. These abbreviations have to do with engine displacement, a term used to measure engine size and power. Displacement is the total volume of space through which the pistons of an engine travel. Displacement is usually expressed in liters. American 4-cylinder cars, for instance, have engines that range from 1.5 to 2.5 liters in size. A 6-cylinder engine may range from 2.5 to 4.5 liters.

In the abbreviation GTO, the "O" stands for "over." A GTO car is a Grand Touring car with an engine that displaces more than 3.0 liters. GTU refers to an engine that is "under" 3.0 liters.

The SCCA, with more than 34,000 members, offers competition for both amateur and professional drivers in these various classes.

GTP competition at Lime Rock Park, Lime Rock, Connecticut.

More than 7,500 drivers compete in the club's amateur racing program. These, as *Car and Driver* magazine once said, are the "little guys" of racing. They pay for racing out of their own pockets. They bring their families and friends to help at the track. Instead of prize money, the winner gets a silver trophy with a car on top.

Of the 2,500 races for amateurs that the SCCA offers each year, the biggest is the Valvoline Road Racing Classic, which decides the national champions. Held in October at Road Atlanta, near Gainesville, Georgia, the Classic brings together well over 500 division champions and high-point qualifiers. They compete for national titles in more than twenty different race classes. These range from tiny showroom stock cars to the hottest Trans-Am machines.

The site couldn't be better. Road Atlanta, *Car and Driver* magazine has said, is so beautiful "it could qualify as a public park." Besides its natural beauty, it offers some of the hairiest twists and turns of any road course in the nation.

Drivers compete, not for cash, but for silver

cups and pewter trays. But don't think the competition is any less intense than it is among top professionals who vie for big money prizes. The finals—or runoffs, as they are called—produce plenty of fender bending and more than their share of multicar crashes.

The three days of competition following the qualifying rounds at Road Atlanta serve as one of racing's foremost training grounds. Dozens of Indy stars first achieved success at the Valvoline Classic.

While the SCCA's schedule of amateur races is the biggest of all race programs, the Club is best known for its series of professional road

Many GTP cars have an exotic look. This is a rotary engine Mazda.

This Buick Somerset is a typical Trans-Am car.

races. These include the Trans-Am (for Trans-American), Can-Am (Canadian-American) and Showroom Stock Sedan series.

In its Trans-Am series, the SCCA offers the best-known and longest-running series of road races in North America. It began life in 1966. At the time, so-called "pony cars" were enjoying great popularity. These included Ford's Mustang, Chevrolet's Camaro, Pontiac's Firebird, and Mercury's Cougar. When the SCCA decided to create a series of races for these celebrated sports sedans, they called it the Trans-Am series.

Trans-Am cars, at 2,600 pounds, are about 1,100 pounds lighter than NASCAR Grand National cars. They are powered by V-8 engines. Some of the larger engines generate 600 horsepower, while the light, smaller-engined cars are rated at as little as 350 horsepower. Top speed is around 180 miles an hour.

In recent years, the Trans-Am circuit has been made up of about fifteen different events, each a 100-miler. They're held in such cities and towns as Riverside, California; Portland, Oregon; Detroit, Michigan; Gainesville, Georgia; and Trois Rivieres, Quebec, Canada.

Cars are not permitted to refuel in a Trans-Am event. Tire changes are rare. Make a pit stop for any reason, in fact, and you're also almost certain to end up a loser.

The driver's championship is decided on the basis of points earned in each race—20 to the winner, 16 for second place, 14 for third, then 12, 11, 10, and so forth, down to one point for 15th place. Normally, 32 cars are entered in a race.

In 1966, the first Trans-Am race was won by Jochen Rindt in an Alfa Romeo. But the next year, American auto makers began to dominate the competition, and they have ever since. The leading models include Chevrolet's Camaros and Corvettes; Ford's Mustangs and Thunderbirds; Lincoln's Mercurys, Capris, and Merkurs; Pontiac's Trans-Ams and Fieros; and Buick's Somersets. As this suggests, the cars that compete resemble the ones the spectators drive to the track.

German and Japanese manufacturers have gotten into the Trans-Am act in recent years. Germany is represented by Porsche's 944s, 924s, and 911s; Japan, by Nissan's 300 ZX Turbos.

Walley Dallenbach, Jim Miller, and Chris Kneifel are among the leading Trans-Am drivers. Not to be overlooked are former Olympic decathlon champion Bruce Jenner and actor Paul Newman. Newman, a veteran Trans-Am driver, pilots a Nissan.

The Can-Am (for Canadian-American) series of races, also sponsored by the Sports Car Club of America, is almost as old as the Trans-Am series. In 1987, it entered its twentieth year of competition.

Like Trans-Am, the Can-Am circuit has served as a proving ground for Indy drivers. Al Unser, Al Unser, Jr., Mario Andretti, Bobby Rahal, and Danny Sullivan all competed on the Can-Am circuit.

The Showroom Stock Sedan series of races dates to 1972. These cars have to be "absolutely" stock. There can be no changes in a car as it comes from the dealer beyond the installation of a roll-bar cage to enclose the driver, competitive-strength seat belts, and a fire extinguisher.

Showroom Stock Sedans compete in endurance races. The race begins when the first car crosses the starting line after the green-

One way that drivers gain the skill and experience necessary for "big league" competition is by driving cars like this one in Skip Barber/Saab Pro Series.

flag signal. It ends when the leader crosses the finish line at the end of the prescribed length of time for the race—four hours, six hours, twelve hours, or twenty-four hours.

The twenty-four hour race, held each year at Nelson Ledges Road Course near Akron, Ohio, is becoming one of the most celebrated events on the SCAA calendar. It's come to be known as "racing's toughest day." The three-driver teams average around 70 miles an hour over the 24-hour period and cover more than 1,600 miles.

In both the amateur and professional race programs, SCCA members do much more than merely drive the cars. They also volunteer to serve as race officials, car inspectors, flaggers, timers, and scorers. Indeed, they do all the tasks that have to be done in putting on a race program.

Scores of other important professional races are sponsored each year by the International Motor Sports Association. All are road racing events.

A Porsche 930S in action in a GT event at Lime Rock, Connecticut.

Buick Hawk, one of the classic prototypes among cars competing on GTP circuit

These include the races in the Camel GT series. Founded in 1971, it offers more than $2.5 million in prize money. These races attract GT cars that offer the very latest in high-tech design. The chassis are produced by Porsche, Lola, March, Ford, Nissan, Jaguar, and BMW. The engines come from Jaguar, Buick, Porsche, Chevrolet, BMW, Nissan, and Ford.

For several years, the Porsche 935 engine dominated the Camel GT series. Indeed, in one year, 1980, the 935 finished one-two-three in all but one event. And in that one exception, the 935 finished one-two. By 1983, however, cars powered by Jaguar, Ford, and Chevrolet engines joined Porsche powerplants in the winner's circle.

The driving talent is the very best. The competitors have included Bob Wollek, three-time winner of the Porsche Cup, Derek Bell and Hans Stuck, World Endurance Champions, and such American standouts as Bobby Rahal, Danny Sullivan, and Al Unser, Jr.

The Kelly American Challenge is another series of races sponsored by IMSA. These bring together mid-size American sedans—Buick Somersets, Oldsmobile Cieras, Chevrolet Camaros, Pontiac Firebirds, and Fords and Dodges.

The Champion Spark Plug Challenge, a third series of races sponsored by IMSA, is for mid-size sedans and also smaller, front-wheel drive sedans. Dodge Daytonas and Chargers, Mazda 623s and 323s, Chevrolet Cavaliers, Honda Preludes, and Pontiac Grand-Ams are among the cars that compete. There are also Volkswagons, Renaults, and Nissans.

The Firestone Firehawk Endurance Championship is the newest series of races sponsored by IMSA. Begun in 1985, it offers ten events, nine of them six hours in length, plus one 24-hour test in the middle of the season. Cars are raced "as delivered" to buyers in automobile showrooms. As this suggests, Firehawk competition puts an emphasis on one's talent as a driver; mechanical skill is secondary.

Year by year, IMSA races have increased in number. They keep offering more prize money and getting greater television coverage. In one recent year, attendance averaged 40,000 people per event. In less than two decades, IMSA has become an important force in American auto racing.

A Porsche 944, driven by Kent Hill of Atlanta, Georgia, competes in a Firestone Firehawk event.

INDEX